Got Some River In Us

Mosaic of the Yazoo-Mississippi Delta

A Collage Long Poem by

Nancy Dafoe

Finishing Line Press
Georgetown, Kentucky

Got Some River In Us

Copyright © 2026 by Nancy Dafoe
ISBN 979-8-89990-353-3 First Edition
All rights reserved under International and Pan-American Copyright Conventions. No part of this book may be reproduced in any manner whatsoever without written permission from the publisher, except in the case of brief quotations embodied in critical articles and reviews.

ACKNOWLEDGMENTS

Got Some River in Us is dedicated to artists, writers, musicians, lyricists, dramatists, photographers, designers, print makers, and illustrators making art about place, about a region and its people, about America; to Leah Maines and FLP for their continued faith in poets experimenting with form and content; to Rosemary James, whose Faulkner competition brought me to an even deeper love of the region; to Joanne Sealy, Faulkner House Books Store Manager, who communicated with me during the COVID-19 pandemic to send me notes and books; to William Faulkner who suggested the Delta was a state of mind from "the lobby of a Memphis, Tennessee, hotel and extend[ing] south to the Gulf of Mexico;" to Greenville, MS native and Chamber of Commerce cheerleader for her state Carolyn Baker; to author and professor James Wiggins for his lectures and writings; to New Orleans writer Sue Sparrow; to my daughters Colette and Nicole Dafoe, always my first readers; to my husband Daniel for taking a trip up the Mississippi River with me; and with deep and special appreciation for Jamie Tate whose remarkable contemporary art inspired me to take this dive into the Yazoo-Mississippi Delta, region and rivers of astounding yet troubled beauty.

Publisher: Leah Huete de Maines
Editor: Christen Kincaid
Cover and Interior Art: Jamie Tate. Tate's art *Return to Avalon* image used with permission from the owners Mike and Betsy Bostic of Greenville, MS. Jamie Tate's cover art *Troubled Waters* used with permission from the owners Colette Dafoe and David Cusano, Maryland.
Author Photo: Parker Stone
Cover Design: Elizabeth Maines McCleavy

Order online: www.finishinglinepress.com
　　　　　also available on amazon.com

Author inquiries and mail orders:
Finishing Line Press
PO Box 1626
Georgetown, Kentucky 40324
USA

Contents

Got Some River in Us

I

Rivers Remember Where They Used to Be 1

II

Shores of Richness and Ruin 11

III

Hard, Hard Birthing of the Blues 21

IV

Seeking Oracles and Preachers 31

V

A Whirling American Comet 41

Notes 51

Bios 57

I

Rivers Remember Where They Used to Be

Long before man, rivers swirled and churned
with wildness, independent without witness.
Their voices soft cool or low rumble rushing—
water swallowed itself, renewing.

Construction of contradictions—
the Yazoo-Mississippi Delta
traced back to Cretaceous
when waters later termed Mississippi
found a shorter route to rising seas,
pulling, depositing glutted soils
in deltaic cycles capturing widening river—
distributary flowing into new complexes
of saline marshes,
nutrient rich, estuarine water—
distilled essence of the not-yet
but to-be American Deep South,
like a later day
Mississippi Bourbon punch.

Some 70 million years ago,
a river surged through embayment
when dinosaurs still roamed
near waters, and dinosaur-like reptiles
swam in waters yet to become the Mississippi.

"Vertebrate material [beneath the river bed] includes bones of turtles and mosasaurs, as well as teeth from extinct sharks and fish, crocodiles, and occasionally hadrosaurs and theropods."[1]

Four million years ago,
river growing to gargantuan breadth,
long before man tried to harness
that heedlessness; river changing
course, rate and volume of flow.

Closer to the Gulf in the Delta,
flat, flat lowlands—
straight-edge horizon;
line bisecting soil and water from sky—
where the idea of a flat Earth
might have first erupted
if it hadn't been misconceived
somewhere else.

"Around 60 million years ago, the Mississippi was collecting water from the Rockies to the Appalachians; by four million years ago, its watershed had extended into Canada, and the Mississippi had grown to an enormous size, carrying four to eight times as much water as it does today."[2]

Millions of years pass unnoticed,
rivers converging. Water once carried
river shrimp, shellfish,
another eon running through.

With man's entrance came naming:
the Great Water roads—
Arkansas, Atchafalaya, Ohio,
and Red Rivers; Tallahatchie,
Leaf, Yalobusha, and Coldwater;
Missouri, Wabash, Big Black,
and Chickasawhay; the Pearl
and Yazoo joining the Mississippi,
who calls all her children home.

Assigning Mississippi, "Proud Mary,"
"Big River," "Old Man River"
long after Indigenous People
called her Misi-ziibi.

"Occasionally, the river floods these places. 'Floods' is the word they use, but in fact it is not flooding; it is remembering. Remembering where it used to be."[3]

Vermillion Bay to Chandeleur Islands,
bounded by Loess bluffs in the "Sipp"
to the east, great river to the west

where land and water meet
in state of flux—
where roads are rivers,
and rivers within rivers:
flooded terrain transformed.

"It was as if the water itself were in three strata, separate and distinct, the bland and unhurried surface bearing frothy scum and a miniature flotsam of twigs and screening as though by vicious calculation the rush and fury of the flood itself."[4]

Contradictions of locus flowing, pulsing;
resplendence born of and in the river;
conversely, flooding wages destruction:
causal dichotomy.

Radiance reflected on waters' ever-changing
surfaces; sights to inspire, river to create
change, to introduce again and again
what is true; no, what is beautiful
yet terrible about the region,
this yet-to-be America.

Yellows, blues, a subterfuge of bluish
color in diffused light streaming,
clouds mirroring running rivers below.

"Land of the loins of the river…it laid down this land…pure soil endlessly deep, dark, and sweet."[5]

Land, diluvial, always under threat
of disappearing in this Delta,
until isolated strips of communities
sprang up, communities where they farm
catfish, build and tear down walls
after storms and in sweltering heat;
hope backwater pumps hold
if the levees fail;
listen late night to blues legends—
bards setting song to alluvial plains,
plains alluvial in song.

"The face of the water, in time, became a wonderful book—a book that was a dead language to the uneducated passenger…delivering its most cherished secrets as clearly as if it uttered them with a voice. And it was not a book to be read once and thrown aside, for it had a new story to tell every day."[6]

Yazoo overflowing while Mississippi
disregards its banks repeatedly,
then perversely dries up in sections
after extended summers of drought—
exposing skeletons of old boats
on river bed,
skeletons of waste laid bare
as water pulls back its cloak.

Vessels run aground, queue of barges,
boats stuck in muck. A massive island
in the middle of the river—
Tower Rock compels those who walk
across what was once water
with second thoughts
about old gods.

Stretches of riverbed looking
like new desert.
A buoy, once used to help
navigate, now choking
in discarded ropes and wires,
castoffs from another line.

With the Mississippi River,
nature has a way
of giving bounty,
showing its showoff self,
its ever-changing canvas—
then revealing scarring wounds,
seen when river shudders, shrinks.
Broken ships at bottom betray bones
of forgotten sideboards,
looking like ribcage
of Goliath slain in another age,

those bones uncovered
along with discarded oil drums;
archeology of the river
finding all manner of refuse
tossed away another day.

Salt-water wedge moves closer
to New Orleans as drought
alters mighty Mississippi and creatures
who depend upon her flow:
Plaquemines Parish now choking—
too deep in the salt.

Wide across Delta wetlands,
rain returns and turns to torrents
of liquid glass.
Lightning strikes looking like
giant spiders' webs
across wide sky, vibrating air,
while rivers rapidly rise
as old order Phoenix—
and Lake Pontchartrain strains,
heaves, feeling limits of man-made
levees, even wetlands know
of drowning.

"The Mississippi River will always have its own way; no engineering skill can persuade it to do otherwise."[7]

Canals, dams, pumps, and levees—
man's ingenious attempts to stem
inevitable tides, temporarily holding
serpentine waters that refuse
to be held back for long—
in one of the fastest sinking
areas in the world;
this land subsidence
with causes both natural
and man-made.

A single house stands surrounded
by embankment of sand, silt,
and clay—like some foreign
ancient fortress;
home and inhabitants long since
discovering nothing is impenetrable—
not land, not property, not structures,
not the human heart,
not a life—not a single life.

Fresh water meets brackish
percolating,
swelling up along ornate columns
and cast-iron gates;
iron balconies rusting in cities—
Natchez, Vicksburg, Ste. Genevieve,
Hickman, Altenburg, Kaskaskia,
Baton Rouge, Cape Giradeau,
Greenville, Venice, New Orleans—
water bubbling up through
sagging wood floors
of modest, Cajun shotgun houses,
around doors of narrow dogtrot abodes,
finding a way even through brick and stucco,
penetrating Creole houses
with intricate ironworks—
feeling decay creeping
like Mr. No-Shoulders.

Left for time, things turn to ruin,
drenched as they are in perpetual
damp and torrid temps:
a boil floating on stagnant surface
even as fresh water promises,
renews, restores, and flows below.

"One who knows the Mississippi will promptly aver—not aloud, but to himself—that ten thousand River Commissions, with the mines of the world at their back, cannot tame that lawless stream, cannot curb it or confine it, cannot say to it, 'Go here, or Go there,' and make it obey; cannot save a shore which it has sentenced; cannot bar its path with an obstruction which it will not tear down, dance over, and laugh at."[8]

River's color palette
continually changing:
once blue, river runs
painted in yellows, greens,
and browns with fertilizer runoff
and climate change testing terminus.
Toxic green algae blooms
thriving, spewing from Earth's caldrons
and machinations of careless man.

Mangroves cut for development release
dangerous carbons they hugged for ages;
maritime shrubs' protection
of green sea turtles,
in their shrinking coastal environs,
rapidly disappearing.

Yet, everywhere in the Delta there is water:
swollen marshes, wide water expanse,
creeks spreading out, and land lost,
lost to the sea.

"The Mississippi River carries the mud of thirty states and two provinces 2,000 miles south to the delta and deposits 500 million tons of it there every year. The business of the Mississippi, which it will accomplish in time, is methodically to transport all of Illinois to the Gulf of Mexico."[9]

Over 2,340 miles of river,
the Mississippi waterway
home to nesting birds
flying through—
largest migration corridor
on the continent—
dabbling gadwalls stirred by herons
and ibis taking flight
from tops of cypress.

Rookeries of wading birds juxtaposed
with colonies of pelicans in mangroves'
dense masses; terns in sea grasses,
shorebirds on sands—
surviving because of these wetlands.

"It seems safe to say that it is also the crookedest river in the world, since in one part of its journey it uses up one thousand three hundred miles to cover the same ground that the crow would fly over in six hundred and seventy-five."[10]

Lands nicknamed "sand-blow,"
"cotton dirt" and "rice land" hang on
by moody fickleness of great river
and weather and man-altered weather.

Towns from Minnesota to Louisiana
named Midnight, Egypt,
and Alligator looming larger in imagination
than their physical size.

Smells of soaked soil staying
indelibly in air;
soybean oil pungent like sour fish—
thick. Lower lands stretched out
on a plumb line
and cotton-covered as summer snow—
"livin' in high cotton now"
with wildflowers tickling senses
beneath unctuous odors of herbicides—
in soil, on skin—
holding on.

"The Mississippi is a just and equitable river; it never tumbles one man's farm overboard without building a new farm just like it for that man's neighbor."[11]

Everything here sounds like water—
leaves in wind, fans whirring,
cars rushing, creatures great and small
gurgling, undercurrents in the blood.

Words like rain falling, splashing—
water pushing with enough force
to sculpt rock, defy attempts
to clear streets after storms;
rush onward, carrying all down,
down
to the Gulf,
where land disappears.

"And in the stillness of the room you heard the roar and howl and crash of the great river whose flood had caught them land shaken them and brought Magnolia Ravenal to bed ahead of her time."[12]

Water simultaneously signifying
death, rebirth.
Water surrounding, seeping
from and into the Delta.
Yazoo-Mississippi Delta:
land and rivers—this Holy Grail,
found and lost again;
found and lost:
region of light and dark,
region of foul racism
and saving grace,
region of new life and violent death,
in continual reminder of defeat
and regeneration:
this Waterland.

II

Shores of Richness and Ruin

So that was how it was and was to be:
shores of richness and ruin—

in a phrase, a storied, profane history,
oft forgotten or dismissed,
a history of colonization
and forced displacement.
Choctaws driven out;
Chickasaw, Creek, and then
Cherokees pushed on the Trail of Tears
all the way to Oklahoma
through the Mississippi Delta—
not relocated peoples
but dislocated into sorrowing
by General Jackson's decree:
Indian Removal Act.

As if white officialdom could justify
what took place: stealing of land
with a quarter of Indigenous Peoples
dying along the way;
women and children buried
in unmarked shallow graves,
politically justified by White men's
tales of Native American violence,
violence that all too often
is the story of subjugated man.

"Violence is a personal necessity for the oppressed...It is not a strategy consciously devised. It is the deep, instinctive expression of a human being denied individuality."[13]

Violent and fertile, fertile and violent—
this Yazoo-Mississippi Delta—
this land of cotton, sugar plantations,
richness and poverty,
inhumanity to man, woman,
and child held in slavery,
forced to build wealth of the few
on their scarred backs.

Not original sin but monumental,
unforgivable National sin:
our collective American history
of privilege for the wealthy;
riches born in horrors of slavery;
a history that is not only our past
but our past continually
imploding present:
how history plants us.

"Poor men did not come to the Delta and make themselves rich; rich men came to the Delta to get richer."[14]

Stories become mythology—
"Devil beatin' his'n wife,"

tale told or sung or drawn in this region
of rich, incongruous rivers
in light of man's attempts
to harness them.

Named by Indigenous Peoples,
the Mississippi, Misi-Ziibi
by the Chippewa;
Great Water by the Algonquin;
ancient water or beyond age—
Occochappo and MishaSpiokni
by the Choctaws; Anishinaabe by the Ojibwe.

Father of Waters named by Zebulon Pike's
military expedition heading up head waters
for Jefferson to map territory—
our White Manifest Destiny
to conquer, pillage, and plunder.

History blending, bleeding,
we hear the claims:
French settlements,
Yazoo Peoples before that,
Natchez even before slaves
chained and stolen
from the African Continent,
from the Caribbean,
to work deep arable soils,
turning cotton red,
making slave holders
"rolling in it."

Man, woman, and child held against
their wills; their bodies belonging
to some other: body owned.
These actions "excused" for profits
wrest from the land and souls—
at odds with rivers' natural course.

"Grief is just so scary.... If we finally begin to cry all those suppressed tears, they will surely wash us away like the Mississippi River."[15]

How native son Richard Wright
equated fear of inevitable flooding
with fear of racist whites in writing
his flood stories, stories of rivers,
and racism overflowing banks—
metaphors for the suffocation
of black men, women, and children
at the hands of slaveholders
and their descendants willing to
deny history and blood.

All in tension with nature,
in tension with the human heart—
disposition of men impelled
by need for survival juxtaposed against
those with great, terrible greed.

"Perhaps that's what all human relationships boil down to: would you save my life? Or would you take it?"[16]

Lands later lost to delinquency
going to railroads and lumber companies.
Irish and German—European immigrants
flooding in like new rivers
that would not be held back.
Later yet, Asian immigrants came
as the Delta rivers rolled on.

This intriguing, vibrant,
but oft-volatile mix
of peoples who sometimes married,
who had children,
yet did not associate
with one another.

"Very few writers understand the complex history and maddening social order of the Mississippi Delta."[17]

The Yazoo-Mississippi Delta—
a marrow place,
yet a region of entrenched poverty
beside another kind of richness:
wealth beside economic stagnation,
strangulation, suffocation for those
who find no escape from an endless
cycle; this country offering a mirror
to the whole of America
that oft refuses to see
its own reflection—
its own culpability in actions.

"People are mostly layers of violence and tenderness wrapped like bulbs, and it is difficult to say what makes them onions or hyacinths."[18]

A place wide and deep with rivers
and tributaries: Yazoo in Mississippi
and the Mississippi River
running the length from Illinois
to the Gulf, stealing,
enriching as it flows.

"The Delta seemed besieged by tangible physical forces as well as moral ones. Flood and malaria were constant companions, and the horrible yellow fever epidemic of 1878 was an indelible element of Delta lore."[19]

With names like Beauregard,
Dutrey, and Slidell, life traced
in open-laced with light windows
and just off dirt roads,
past pecan orchards,
into city streets lengthening
even as new campsites set up
along shores of ruin—
upwelling again and again.

"The Delta story for a larger society in which material successes frequently counted for more than moral failure and human environmental costs were all too often no object at all"[20]

Wood, iron, and stucco buildings
capsized in hurricanes and tornadoes,
then fires, deepening red
until even skies caught fire.
Yazoo City burned to the ground,
then inhabitants spoke of moans
coming from the river—
in this ghost-inhabited place.

"[L]and defined by the blues music that once seemed to wail across
tall flood-protection levees and every furrow plowed into the dirt"[21]

Not even a bufflehead's guttural call
or screech from a catbird diverts
the mind caught in sizzling,
crackling sounds
of conflagration
in rush of hot, high winds
blowing down to black
where smoke destroys color.

In a locale where color line
is set in stone
and blood,
in history repeating itself:
sacred and profane in both fire
and recurrent flood.

"He felt that he was caught between two forces: the river and the
white man; and that both were trying to destroy him."[22]

Manifestations of fear and violence,
and heat not yet cooled
outsized beyond the Civil War
that lasted past all boundaries
of time and historical texts,
written by those wielding
power, not truth.
Emmitt Till's murder in LeFlore County
stirred barely buried guilt
like lynchings

in hill country
just beyond the rivers.

"Then the light changed the water, until all about them the woods in the rising wind seemed to grow taller and blow inward together and suddenly turn dark. The rain struck heavily. A huge tail seemed to lash through the air and the river broke in a wound of silver."[23]

Wounds felt if not seen walking
to the National Cemetery in Chalmette
where they lingered
among weathered crypts,
discolored bricks, cement glaze
slowly breaking down
whites and grays,
black mildew adorning tombs
like painted inflections.

Surprising vibrancy in figurines
of the Virgin Mary
secreted in cryptic enclosures;
wrought iron lace of railings,
embedded wrought iron chairs,
relics of beautiful corrosion
haunting in this place.

Passing pirate's National Park,
irony only now noted
over Jean Lafitte being honored
for coming to the aid of a racist
Andrew Jackson in the bloody battle
of New Orleans all those years ago.

Between land and water—
always water—
between Decatur and Canal Streets,
between the Mississippi
and Lake Pontchartrain,
a group of children posed for a photo
ten years before Katrina blew through.

Running onto a stone bridge waving,
their multicolored coats reflected
in water, children shouted
for the image maker's attention.

"I would hurl words into the darkness and wait for an echo…to create
a sense of hunger for life that gnaws in us all."[24]

Photograph of children,
a rainbow reflection
over bridge, with finely woven moss
hanging from tree limbs in embrace.

"The Mississippi Delta is not always dark with rain. Some autumn
mornings, the sun rises over Moon Lake, or Eagle, or Choctaw, or
Blue, or Roebuck, all the wide, deep waters of the state, and when it
does, its dawn is as rosy with promise and hope as any other."[25]

Only years later,
after devastation
of Hurricane Katrina,
would a Northern photographer,
an outsider, a wanderer,
take in the wonder
and beauty of the Delta region,
then recall the moment
long later, in reflection—
struck by divine grace of children;
black and white print
revealing optimism
even as brightly colored coats
were transposed
into shades of gray—

when news of Katrina's wrath
swirled, spreading like flooding
rivers into other lands.

How those eight-year-olds—
now grown—
had weathered storm-infested waters,

political embroilment,
displacement and derision,
resulting in unheeded cries for help.

"It's not enough to celebrate the ideals that we're built on, liberty and justice and equality for all. Those just can't be words on paper, the work of every generation is to make those words mean something, concrete in the lives of our children. And we won't get there as long as kids in Baltimore or Ferguson or New York or Appalachia or the Mississippi delta or the Pine Ridge reservation believe that their lives are somehow worthless."[26]

Eyes with hope even in trepidation
in citizens of a city built between
waters and dreams.
Eyes with hope
in Privation's children
in the richest land,
richest country—
children of the French and Spanish,
the Indigenous Peoples,
from African countries
and Caribbean islands,
the Creoles, Scotts Irish,
later yet, Filipinos
Chinese, Vietnamese
and Lebanese—those seeking
solace in a troubled past
and troubled present—
land of this volatile, vibrant locale.

Delta region in America—
land with 400 billionaires,
paltry millionaires laid barren
beside wishful, exuberant dreams
of Poverty's children.

III

Hard, Hard Birthing of the Blues

If there is a Greek god to favor
the Yazoo-Mississippi Delta,
it would be Dionysus:
sensual, fertile but wholly drunken,
dancing to music, poetry,
and visual art
across farm fields,
in streets and swamps.

Bottle trees line rivers reflecting
brittle, brilliant light in life
juxtaposed beside shade.

Art, music, words shine on this region—
creative gifts to the country and world.

"I don't want to make somebody else. I want to make myself."[27]

Cradle of music, birthplace
of Delta blues:
Charley Patton, Howlin' Wolf,
Robert Johnson playing all night
in this intersection of peoples
and ache and want and injustice—
Johnson said to have sold his soul
to the Devil for the gift
of his black velvet song,
playing like serving time.

"Like his clerical counterpart, the bluesman was a key figure, symbolic of a communal culture…Like the preacher, the bluesman entertained his audiences by expressing deeply felt, shared emotions in a manner that made him more than an entertainer."[28]

Ishman Bracey recording, getting
it down, recording so it would
not be forgot. Kid Bailey
with his disappearing act
melding into Willie Brown,
by some accounts, heard
but almost forgotten except
in those "Rowdy Blues,"
and Floyd Lee migrating
like a colorful bird,
only heading North, not South,
to New York City with
Lee's "Mean Blues"
in mean streets—
all far more than entertainers,
more than crooners, gifted musicians

carrying the heavy weight
of history,
of suffering of people
in lyrics and song.

Dockery Farms once plantation
where single cabins fell into ruin;
where slave owners tore apart families—
where even the soil greedily
drank up that depth of sorrowing
spilled out in song,
in that slide guitar weeping
for babies,
for women,
for men who grew old
without families without, without,
without freedom.

"Somebody done nailed us on the cross," lamented elderly, dispossessed Sunflower County tenant. "Don't know who it is, but I believe it's the government."[29]

"Whatever inclinations toward morality and justice white leaders in Tallahatchie County may have shown in the immediate aftermath of the killing [of Till] were overwhelmed by their resentment of the criticism they received from the northern press and black activist groups. With civil rights pressures beginning to swell, justice took a back seat to white unity and supremacy."[30]

Land where Rock & Roll arose—
where Elvis and B.B. King
were Kings, the Queen-in-waiting—
Anna Mae Bullock
ascending from the Riverland
as Tina Turner, that girl
from Nutbush, Tennessee,
who went to school in Brownsville,
and attained great heights.

"As a form the blues is an autobiographical chronicle of personal catastrophe expressed lyrically"[31]

Graceland in Memphis where the ghost
of Elvis still roams
before a pilgrimage of lovers,
both true and false, migrates
toward the realm of their prophet.

This land home to Arcadian
or Cajun sounds
with their spoons, cellos,
and harmonicas buzzing
in rhythm while a sea of dancers
move in cadence at watering holes—
with names like Red's and Smoot's
and Walnut Street and Club Ebony—
awaiting Zydeco button accordions
or Lucious singing the blues
in not-so-sacred juke joints.

"The blues was just everywhere in the Mississippi Delta. It was mostly black sharecroppers living there, and there was a lot of blues around. Sometimes the guys would sing the blues in the fields, working."[32]

Muddy Waters
and John Lee Hooker echoing
river's flow—tears building before
rage in response to white hot racism
and perpetual inhumanity
of man to human.

Against that backdrop of night
and love and injustice,
cicadas—
that great Southern noisy brood—
beat their tymbals to announce
a metrical ticking,
rasping lyric
beside that of a lone man's
or woman's or child's.

"That Mississippi sound, that Delta sound is in them old records. You can hear it all the way through."[33]

The kind of song to melt you,
pull away the detritus
and leave you raw
or suddenly joyful
or remembering,
remembering
and sorrowing.

In New Orleans, jazz was born,
a difficult birth, a bewildering,
gloriously strange baby
crawling up out of the belly
fully formed:
clarinets, horns, and the sixth
interrupting
with a new tone found beside
melodies in pianos
and in hotels and colorful dives;
jumping out in the streets
where Doreen Kitchens
held her clarinet like a lost lover,
squeezing high notes
out of impossibility.

"Every time I close my eyes blowing that trumpet of mine, I look right into the heart of good old New Orleans. It has given me something to live for."[34]

City torn apart every few years
by hurricanes, tornadoes, and floods,
then resurrected after receding waters,
followed by political conflagration
but found again and again,
rising like Dionysus, like Phoenix
or invasive vine that keeps coming
back in a thick air
of mystery and grandeur
to sensual,
repeated dissolution.

Delta spirit of resurrection,
no more so than in flood-razed,
continually reborn New Orleans;
the French Quarter where a bower
of bougainvillea establishes
dominion in hidden gardens,
near rot-catching rims
of wooden benches,
window frames
and shutters marked
by watermarks while speaking
another language
of lush exuberance,
of life in this otherworldly city:
city of water, vibrancy,
and decay.

Creativity in music,
in paintings, in literary abundance,
in theatrical staging and performance—
Blanche forever coming out
of the shadows depending
upon the "kindness of strangers."[35]

Performances found in poets' words,
in movement and barely audible sighs,
in sounds, tastes—tongue expectant—
feasts of culinary delight
like no other part of the country.

Yet home to abject, reigning Poverty—
bounded by neighboring, absurd wealth—
children in deep distress.
and longing.

"Men's bodies litter my family history," Jesmyn Ward wrote in her memoir Men We Reaped. "The pain of the women they left behind pulls them from the beyond, makes them appear as ghosts. In death, they transcend the circumstances of this place that I love and hate all at once and become supernatural."[36]

Supernatural intensifying through life
and loss voiced in piercing high notes
of a saxophone player holding
out a hat round the corner of an old hotel
where a homeless man is cocooned
in moldy blanket
in mid-day high heat.

Vieux Carre of hidden gardens—
both literal and metaphoric—
always under threat;
the past not beneath nor behind
present
but ever present.

"The past is never dead. It's not even past."[37]

If you stopped recording
human experience after New Orleans
and the Yazoo-Mississippi Delta,
you would still know
humanity's potential for artistic achievements
and tragedies, monumental losses,
deep desires, and exotic,
passionate, troubling loves.

When first governor William Claiborne
called the city "ungovernable" out of lack
of understanding, insult now reads
as tribute to the spirit of the people.
In New Orleans, you know
music and eternal love in your being,
following ingenuity and eccentricity
in connections through every art form
and every endeavor down to blood, bone.

"America has only three cities: New York, San Francisco, and New Orleans. Everywhere else is Cleveland." Then giving his character his words, "Don't you just love those long rainy afternoons in New Orleans when an hour isn't just an hour, but a little piece of eternity dropped into your hands, and who knows what to do with it?"[38]

Drama in the Delta with dancers,
trumpets and guitars in the streets;
with swamp men hunting gators.
While poets and singers spout verse
in multiple, musical tongues;
with maenads running through
wetlands or into cities,
holding gods and demons within.
Mardi Gras, carnival,
ritual and rites of passage
in this hot, sultry land.
Rhythms of its people, even more
than its guitars, accordions, drums
thumping life—
incessant and insistent—
where fertility deities idle and stay
to sleep then wake to sleep—
slowing to another day.

"The Blues is a lowdown shakin' chill"[39]

Impossible, incredible cuisine:
like fried buffalo fish sandwiches,
bass and "river cat" with comeback sauce,
jambalaya and gumbo,
and fried pickles, slug burgers,
and Flossie's Mississippi tamales,
crawfish, andouille sausage,
fried chicken and etouffee,
candied yams and collard greens,
sorghum molasses on pancakes,
Mississippi mud
and mile high meringue pie –
indulgences even before
arriving at this cuisine,
music, and word Capital.

"There is no place on Earth even remotely like New Orleans. Don't even try to compare it to anywhere else,"[40]

Enigmatic New Orleans,
like the Yazoo-Mississippi Delta itself—
Spanish, French, Irish,
Indigenous Peoples,
Caribbean, African descendants,
immigrants and native born—
making time in the Delta,
clamoring Land,
corrupted, enriched
with Arcadians, Cajuns, Creoles
building again—
black and white—continually
confounding notions
of race and culture.

Cities and towns arose along
rich velvet wetlands:
Greenville—something about
that city that produced more writers
per acre—words flowing like rivers
surrounding them:
Ste. Genevieve, Kaskaskia,
Altenburg, Wittenburg, Cairo,
Cleveland, Memphis, Vicksburg,
Natchez, Clarksdale, Cape Girardeau,
Tunica, Hickman, Helena, Venice,
Baton Rouge, and New Orleans
refusing to be swallowed whole
by waters even as they gasp
and gulp for air.

Rites buried then unearthed
in funeral dances—
a little drunk, a little mad,
a little proud but gloriously
dripping with dew and sweat—
sweat pouring over dancers moving
sensually, sexually
below even the level of the sea.

"As long as New Orleans exists, it will attract the imaginative, the creative, the adventurous, and the soulful people of the world."[41]

Mississippi Delta glowing in darkness
and near blinding mid-day light,
quality of sunlight burnished
then ablaze.

IV

Seeking Oracles and Preachers

Natural world of the Delta
entering the supernatural—
unwilling to expel inner demons,
looking for saving saints—
paranormal accepted in gestures
of weeping angels
or graves dug for imagined witches
beside Christian crosses

converging on island sacraments
in ancestor worship,
veneration of deities
to give life to Voodoo-Catholicism,
new World, Southern Baptists
round every corner.

"Its cultural diversity is woven into the food, the music, the architecture, even the local superstitions. It's a sensory experience on all levels and there's a story lurking around every corner."[42]

Voices raised in song of shared hymns
but not shared churches,
the Delta's spiritual claims' varied versions
of what is sacred;
what is segregated.
Segregated and not equal in equal
measure. Justifying injustice
in tradition as finely tuned
as a Northern Yankee's.

Oral traditions
and measured cadence
as layered, overflowing
their boundaries
like surrounding rivers.
Bluesman singing his soul
and his manhood into spiritual
hymn while questions
of and inversions about
Providence swirling
like muddy waters.

Christian churches bear the crosses
of those sacrificed
not for original sin
but the ever-present one
born in slavery—
its legacy lingering,
smoldering,
sometimes into conflagration.

[Morrison] "makes strong connections between Black suffering and Christ's own, especially in *Beloved* and *The Bluest Eye*…Morrison's theology is one of the Passion: of scarred bodies, public execution, and private penance."[43]

"This is not a story to pass on,"[44]
Toni Morrison wrote in irony,
retelling the story of slavery
in America as of utmost importance:
one to be recognized
and remembered
in rememory.

Even a finally sung hymn
in a white dress
with carved angels
at the alter won't wash
it all away.

"The ritual act of immersion carries the hope of renewal and freedom, ideas that have driven African-American spirituality."[45]

Beyond the churches
and organized religions,
"unchurched preachers" like Baby Suggs,[46]
"just strange stuff,"[47]
and a high priestess in the street—
decorated in colorful rags
and gaudy bangles—
sits at a booth in Jackson Square
to tempt passersby, bringing them
into her bountiful fold,
spouting futures her customers
want to see, reshaping experience
into pseudo cohesion.

"The tradition of Southern oratory includes roaring campaign speeches from the back of a pickup truck as well as "fire and brimstone" preaching at a backwoods church revival."[48]

A tall man in an orange turban
wearing oblong, dangling earrings,
reads a woman's palm
at a makeshift table of boxes
covered with blood red cloth,
while Miss Stacey reads a nightmare
and smokes, waiting for clients
at her Tarot and Palm Reading
table spread with black garment
dotted with tiny white stars.
She came from the North
long ago and stayed beyond
tourist season,
believing
she could see more clearly
in a southern light.

"Cause you can love the Delta
and see it every day and not see it,"
she said.
Or you can hold back before entering—
eyes wide open, recognizing where
you have always been.

"Above all, Mississippi, even more than much of the American South, is a land of evangelical Protestants. Baptists dominate numerically, followed by Methodists and other evangelical groups…Religion has played significant, even crucial, roles in almost all of the major issues in Mississippi history."[49]

Religion down by the watering holes,
in hotels, in rural cabins
and Creole cottages;
in historic mansions
and townhouses of the Faubourg Marigny,
and in streets named Bourbon and Canal,
Royale and Esplanade,
the homeless wrap themselves
in the heat of midday
wearing a hat,
palm extended—
their misshapen boots worn thin.

Sightseers enter in droves
to take it all in,
find something,
more than something—
they were looking for.
Small doses suggested
because too much of a good thing—
too much knowledge
and too much feeling—
too much desire
can be dangerous, they decide,
but dip in a toe then two,
dance and drink
until the lights go out.

They look about,
drawn to the promise
of mystery,
drawn to excess for a night
yet unsure if the attraction
is safe enough for them to engage
as the locals laugh and smoke,
drink their breakfasts while watching
a boy kiss an aging woman
with abandon.

"Our too-young and too-new America, lusty because it is lonely, aggressive because it is afraid, insists upon seeing the world in terms of good and bad, the holy and the evil, the high and the low, the white and the black; our America is frightened of fact, of history, of processes, of necessity. It hugs the easy way of damning those whom it cannot understand, of excluding those who look different, and it salves its conscience with a self-draped cloak of righteousness."[50]

Warding off despair,
Red Velvet reads rough or soft palms
while Maman You on Dumaine Street
frightens at first, then excites
those passing, as well as those
who stop to listen,
while Marie on Chartres Street
expertly strokes slender fingers

as she lays out cards;
her hair beautifully braided
with colorful beads;
her wrists decorated
with jangling bracelets
extending
all the way up her arms
as high as musical notes.
Marie is singing as she
reads the future,
and it sounds like a hymn
to some who enter.

"The naked will to power seemed always to walk in the wake of a hymn."[51]

Bayou Baptist preachers
Turners and Carraways;
Evangelical Protestants of Mississippi,
Missionary Baptists diverging
from Southern Baptists
like a fork in the river.

"Toward the church they thronged with slow sabbath deliberation, the women and children went on in, the mend stopped outside and talked in quiet groups until the bell ceased ringing, then they too entered."[52]

Disciples of Christ and the white
Christian women who wrote eloquently
of pro-slavery as if such an abomination
fit neatly between the well-worn
pages of a Bible,
sanctioning perversity.

"Others developed biblical justifications for racial segregation and encouraged the burning of churches that harbored activists."[53]

Church life entangled with politics
and social life until organizing
symbols could be felt
not just heard,

separating black from white,
separating and segregating even
while nodding along the lines
of good day, a smile as broad
as the 'Sipp.
Even while children of mixed
races step out into the sun.

"Religion has played crucial roles in Mississippi's musical and literary traditions, whether as inspiration or sometimes as the subject of frustration."[54]

Midnight Churches resurrect
the sleeping.
Full Gospel Churches
call out the devil;
the Reverends Wright and Wilson—
"sanctified preachers,"
sons of the former
Colonel in the Confederate
army
turned preacher man,
demanding Deacons
send for the best.

Full-throated singing raises the rafters;
black and white lines sharply drawn
in the way they raise outstretched arms
to their God. Simple white structures
for Pastor John and Pastor Kinsey
or Brother Vaughn.

"White opponents of civil rights called on religion in multiple ways. Some tried to avoid civil rights concerns, saying the role of the church involved spiritual issues and not every-day secular questions. Others developed biblical justifications for racial segregation and encouraged the burning of churches that harbored activists."[55]

Talk of "consecrated blood"
as common on a Wednesday
as on a Sunday.

Religion mixing into the life,
the culture, the song,
the literature, the cadence
of the day and night.

"[R]eligion itself was for [William] Faulkner enduring and inescapable [in his literature]."[56]

"Church Mothers" for hard times
as well as the good but,
especially, for the hard times.

Fifteen children in a line for church
from one family, twelve in another.
Family from the ones who let you
sleep on their back porches,
open their doors in the middle
of the night when your eyes
bleed and your hair runs off.
Those who are blessed.

"Here, family has always been a mutable concept. Sometimes it encompasses an entire community, which meant that C.J. also slept on the sofa in Rob's living room and the sofa in Pot's living room, though he was not related to them."[57]

Chanted sermons in the "Bible Belt,"
spiritual longing,
fundamentalist oratory;
Catholic chants, voices
lining out in hymns;
singing conventions definitive.

"The organ strains come rich and resonant through the summer night, blended, sonorous, with that quality of abjectness and sublimation, as if the freed voices themselves were assuming the shapes and attitudes of crucifixions, ecstatic, solemn, and profound in gathering volume…as though death were the boon, like all Protestant music."[58]

Parishes and storefront churches partake;
ritual baptisms once down by the river—
still separate and unequal
except "before the Lord."

"As late as the 1950s, river submersion was common in both African- and Anglo-American Protestant churches but continues today primarily among African Americans."[59]

Never forgetting how white supremacy
played "all" their cards while holding
five Aces.

Church-going and politics
like a fine gumbo.
Ballot boxes lost over the years
would fill a stadium of sinners
asking for salvation.

Hands and voices rise in unison
while Mama Lou reads her cards
round another corner to a young
black boy named Richard
who will write the sins
of their fathers.
"I feel my hell a-risin' every day. Someday it'll burst this levee and wash the whole wide world away."[60]

Near St. Louis Cathedral,
an artist draws souls on paper,
knows quality of light tricked by rivers—
knows yellows not yellow
and blues not blue—
as Lulu adjusts her red glass ball
on mock pewter stand before reading
remnants at the bottom of a cup of tea—
pronouncing that we all hold
the same fate
while hoping, always wishing,
now praying
for eternity.

V

A Whirling American Comet

Do rivers remember what they carried?
Who crossed them?
Rode their flow all the way down
to the mouth?
If they remember where they were
before man, do they remember
what man has done?

Below the soil, there is water.
There is history.

A cockspur coral tree
exotic as it unfolds its flowering
behind a red brick, Garden Townhouse
with its rusting iron gate: decay defining
beauty in this microcosm.

"Dead trees shrouded in kudzu vines reared up like old women. Down and out at last and onto the vast prodigal plain of the Delta, stretching away misty and fecund into the October haze. The land hummed and simmered in its own richness."[61]

Mandevilla flowering vine
trumpets arrival,
winding a vertical path of pink, red,
and apricot flowers under hot sun;
aerial rootlets and clinging vines—
tendrils trailing;
Confederate Jasmine—
carrying that symbolic, torturous naming—
winds its way up trellis, mailboxes, walls.
Invasive black locust tree deeply furrowed
with age and all it has seen
by dusty roadsides.
Fragrant weedy Morningglories
cropping up in soybean and cotton fields.

"For our soil, very dark brown creamy and sweet-smelling, was built up slowly…in its solemn task of cleansing the continent."[62]

Land losses both man-made
and natural mark wetlands
in which ghosts are said to roam.

Mississippi artist attaching cloth rags
to paper with oil paints,
this amalgamation,
this mixed media art
capturing energy,

creating quality of luster—
white and gold brushstrokes
punctuated by a deep red
palate of the Yazoo-Mississippi Delta—
intense color, glinting shaft
nearly blinding
under a sun unmasked
by any sheltering clouds,
painting not of water but suggestion:
structures and rooflines falling away
in artistic license or symbols of poverty,
giving over to merging gold oils,
particles of color layering
on white intensity
until skies become red or black.

"Lucille, who looked white, knew the rules of segregation, but her family never really followed them. That had to change when she arrived in the Delta."[63]

Light and shadows moving in the way
in which even time stretches
and pulls at a different pace
in this river land.

"The Delta seemed to have captured for posterity the essence of the troubling but nonetheless intriguing, historical legacy of the Old South."[64]

In the night skies outside cities,
the Delta breaks open
into constellations
of thousands of stars
punctuating the firmament.
Genesis in violence:

"Economic, political, and social forces that have swept across the American landscape… have actually converged in the Mississippi Delta."[65]

This storied land and these great waters—
Delta some 200 miles long
and seventy miles wide—
reach well past
man-made boundaries,
evidenced in its
"capacity to provide literary as well as a musical window on American society"[66]

This deep land
and these elongated waters—
all pure poetry of the divine
sleeping with the damned—
all birthed like the nation formed
from stars and celestial objects
propelled in generative explosions;
destructive and regenerative forces
from dying stars,
clouds of hot gasses.
Exoplanets obscured by brilliance
seen from the changing banks
of a flooding river below.

"An immense plate being slid over the ground, shallow, opaque, innocent looking, flecked with foam and littered with chicken coops and fence rails."[67]

Artist's brushstrokes'
offer high notes
of man's temporal existence,
suggest the natural and man-made
world juxtaposed,
as well as edifices
and sometimes sorry structures
disappearing into green golds,
and orange while a flock
of white birds flies overhead.

Art capturing breath
of those lost
and those who will be lost
in the still hot air.

Writers inhabiting words
living in the Delta
or passing through
like the migrating, wading birds—
painterly and remembered
after closing their texts,
gazing up at the heavens
where artists recreate the land
and rivers again.

"A strange and detached fragment thrown off by the whirling comet that is America."[68]

Blazing comet that is the Delta,
altering, unforgettable
but destructive.

Yazoo-Mississippi Delta
that is home to
birdlife and allegators
canebrake rattlesnakes,
amongst spider lilies,
cypress, and cattails taking root.
Elusive panther
nearly having disappeared,
lumbering black bear quick
to turn and run, avoiding man
and gator.
Sawgrass marshes
home to, "Twenty-foot and not
an inch less," he said,
describing encounter
on his back step.
"Near took my arm clean off.
Fixin' to go now."
Tales told and embellished
with the telling.

"Once the domain of moccasins, bears, alligators, and panthers."[69]
Mythology in knowing, no, sensing
the unreachable,
that metaphorical advance guard

of minds[70] out across the Delta.
Faulkner observing an army
of ants in a flood of words
deep and layered as the Earth:

"Following undisturbed and unaware its appointed course and serving
its Lilliputian end, like a thread of ants between the rails on which an
express train passes, they [the ants] as unaware of the power and fury
as if it were a cyclone crossing Saturn."[71]

Yazoo-Mississippi Delta inspiring
writer's reflection, words pulled
out of some deep recess,
woven into story, into song
from the land and waterscape,
from the convoluted history
from the geography and geology.

"The Delta is like my own Sargasso Sea, a liminal space of mystery and
madness where my thoughts move between the darkness of the past
and the light that can be found in nature."[72]

Artist noting in swaths of color:
natural world's unconditional offering:
Honeysuckle, cardinal and trumpet
creepers, jasmine, wisteria, and porcelain
berry vines beautifully choking
other plants on their paths.

"The man walked up and down in the darkness of the water oaks,
emerging now and then under the street light, which shed a weak
yellow drizzle. The boy sat on the steps between the azaleas and
watched."[73]

And in watching,
observing, and knowing
where we have been
in this land that is both
mythic and literal in translation
along our fault lines.

"Most of the people here are kin. It is something that the 'Black' people will talk about among themselves, the way our families intertwine and feed one another, and it is something that 'White' people will speak about among themselves, but it something that we rarely speak to each other about, even when those on both sides of the color divide share the same last name."[74]

Called lazy,
these twining, woody vines
take advantage of any structure
to feed on the glow of sunlight
like daytime vampires.

"[O]ne could reasonably argue that the Delta underlies everything in Mississippi—the politics, the economy, the culture, the sense of native identity—so of course it shows up in Yoknapatawpha County, if one knows where to look and listen carefully for it."[75]

The Yazoo-Mississippi Delta
as distinctive
as homemade gumbo,
as satisfying as cracked open oysters,
crawfish etouffee, and po'boys on the side.

"She showed us she loved us the only way she knew how beyond providing a home…She cooked huge pots of gumbo, beef and vegetables, pork chops, mashed potatoes, red beans and rice, pecan candy…and yellow sheet cakes—"[76]

Delta as imbued with our lust
and loves as a python's embrace;
imbued with our violence
as a lynching at midnight.
As distinctive or as misshapen
as bald cypress tacked to brick building
mysteriously holding together
for generations of Creoles hanging on
until the end even of myths,
stories flooding into history
even after they are forgotten.

"Mississippi blood is different. It's got some river in it. Delta soil, turpentine, asbestos, cotton poison. But there's strength in it, too. Strength that's been beat but not broke."[77]

Soaked wood on shacks pealed
away with a fingernail, soft wood
all the way through to rot.
Termites working on the rest.

Loose floorboards threatening,
not an apparition but the condition
of man, woman, and child standing
in a place that promises to fall away
or drop sudden with footfalls
while waterways converge then diverge
into spines below disappearing soils;
while songs rise up from the belly,
from the lungs in repeated rebirth.

Artists painting and writers writing,
songsters starting low in building
to crescendo—
looking for truth in altered light—
always with waters running through.

"The Delta was a land of excess. The hot sun, the torrential rains, the savage caprices of the unpredictable river. The fecund earth, the startlingly rapid growth of vegetation, the illimitable flat plains, and the vast dome of heaven arching over them."[78]

The Delta symbol
of America writ large;
America writ mean
in nearly every sense of the word,
except "average."

"There's so much that you can learn about the world, and I would say about this country, from studying what Mississippi writers have done and written about this place, which I think telescopes onto our larger national issues, and even some of our larger international ones."[79]

America embodied in the eye
of the Delta, in the eye of the hurricane,
breathtaking sunrise
and violent storm
passing through, promising return
in the weather and metaphor.

"Years before the rest of the world, the people of the Delta tasted the bittersweet of modern alienation so that the blues of those days ring true for all of us now."[80]

Defying attempts to define it,
bound it, limit its scope
prove largely academic
but without meaning to the
people, the region, the pace
of the land and rivers.

"It's about us working together. It's about us doing what needs to be done in society today to make sure that our children are actually making progress."[81]

Rivers acknowledges no progress
only changing course.

"Waterways, swampways, woodways, coils within coils, so plain but cunning, so serpentine in its involutions around the heart."[82]

Beneath a vast arching dome—
no longer mere visitor
passing through but one in the blood—
like the river,
remembering where we came from,
remembering we are greatly water,
remembering we were carried
in the womb in mostly water—
we all got some River Delta in us.

Got some powerful guilt in us.
Got some magical creation in us.
Got some strange rhythm in us.

Got some kind a religion in us.
Got some dense nescience in us.
Got some old wisdom in us.
Got some vile hate in us.
Got some deep love in us.
Got the Delta in us.
Got some river in us.
Got some river in us.
Got some river in us.

Notes

1 "The Cretaceous in Mississippi," *The Paleontology Portal.* Time and Space, University of California Museum of Paleontology, National Science Foundation, usgs.gov website, June 27 2024.

2 Dean Klinkenberg, "The 70-Million-Year-Old History of the Mississippi River," *Smithsonian Magazine*, September 2020, 1, ¶5, https://www.smithsonianmag.com/science-nature/geological-history-mississippi-river-180975509/.

3 Toni Morrison, "The Site of Memory," *Inventing the Truth*, edited by William Zinsser, Ed., Houghton Mifflin, (New York, 1995). In addition to the quotation cited, the title of the first section of this poem is a paraphrase of Morrison's original commentary comparing rivers and memory.

4 William Faulkner, *The Wild Palms*, Vintage International, (New York, First Edition, 1995).

5 David L. Cohn, *Where I Was Born and Raised*, (Boston: Houghton Mifflin, First Edition, 1948), 26.

6 Mark Twain, "Two Ways of Seeing a River" from *The Complete Works of Mark Twain* (Illustrated Edition): *Novels, Short Stories, Memoir, Travel Books, Letters, Biography, Articles & Speeches: The Adventures of Tom Sawyer & Huckleberry Finn, Life on the Mississippi, Yankee in King Arthur's Court*, p.6903, e-art now.

7 Mark Twain, *Eruption*, Edited by Bernard DeVoto.

8 Mark Twain, *Life on the Mississippi*. Memoir. 1883.

9 Charles Kuralt, CBS journalist, *The Columbus Dispatch*, Dale Gnidovec, "Geology: Tiny zircon crystals help trace the birth of the mighty Mississippi" (dispatch.com, November 11 2018.)

10 Mark Twain. *Life on the Mississippi*. Memoir. 1883.

11 Mark Twain, *Life*.

12 Edna Ferber, "Showboat."

13 Richard Wright. *Native Son,* 1939, pg. 45.

14 Phillip Gordon, "The Delta and Yoknapatawpha: The Layering of Geography and Myth in the Works of William Faulkner," Center for the Study of Southern Culture, University of Mississippi, Online, 28 November 2016. ¶ 23.

15 Anne Lamont, *Small Victories: Spotting Improbable Moments of Grace*, Riverhead Books. First Edition, 2014.

16 Toni Morrison, *Song of Solomon*, Knopf Double Day Publishing, Vintage, Reprint, 2004.

17 John Grisham, Editorial review of Steve Yarbrough's novel *Safe From the Neighbors,* January 26, 2010.

18 Eudora Welty, *Delta Wedding*. First Edition, 1946.

19 James C. Cobb, *The Most Southern Place on Earth, The Mississippi Delta and the Roots of Regional Identity*, Oxford University Press, (NYC, 1992), 317.

20 James C. Cobb, *The Most Southern Place on Earth*.

21 W. Ralph W. Eubanks, "Mississippi Delta: Returning Home to Its Haunted Past." *Outside*. Online. 8 June 2023, ¶ 9.

22 Richard Wright, "Down by the Riverside." 79.

23 Eudora Welty, "The Wide Net," (183) *The Collected Stories of Eudora Welty*. Harcourt, Inc. Orlando, 1980.

24 Richard Wright, *Black Boy*, Harper Perennial Modern Classics, 2008.

25 Lewis Nordan, *Wolf Whistle* (149). Algonquin Books of Chapel Hill, 1993.

26 Barack Obama, "Inaugural Address," 21 January 2013. Inaugural Address by President Barack Obama whitehouse.gov (archives.gov)

27 Toni Morrison, *Sula*, Vintage, Reprint edition, (June 8, 2004).

28 Cobb, *The Most Southern Place on Earth*, 287.

29 James C. Cobb, *The Most Southern Place on Earth* (Oxford Press, 1992), 271.

30 Cobb, *The Most Southern Place on Earth*, 219.

31 Ralph Ellison, in James C. Cobb, *The Most Southern Place on Earth*. 315.

32 Mose Allison, Mose Allison Quotes, Quote.org. accessed January 7, 2025.

33 Muddy Waters. All Great Quotes, Classic Literature Study Guides, Online, accessed January 7, 2025.

34 Louis Armstrong in *Stowaway Magazine,* Kaytee Johnson. New Orleans Jazz. 29 April 2020.

35 Tennessee Williams, *Streetcar Named Desire*, Paperback edition. Signet. 1986.

36 Jesmyn War, *Men We Reaped, A Memoir*, Bloomsbury, (New York, 2013), 14.

37 William Faulkner, *Requiem for a Nun*. Vintage (New York, 1975).

38 Tennessee Williams, *A Streetcar Named Desire*. Paperback edition. Signet. 1986

39 Robert Johnson, "Preachin' Blues" lyrics.

40 Anthony Bourdain in "There is No Place Like New Orleans," Melissa Rach, Globetrotters, 2023

41 Tom Piazza, *Why New Orleans Matters*. Harper Perrenial (2015).

42 Ruta Sepetys, quoted in *New Orleans French Quarter: The Incomplete Edition*, March 27, 2015, https://photoremedy.me/2015/03/27/new-orleans-french-quarter-the-incomplete-edition/.

43 Toni Morrison, *Critique*. Nick Ripatrazone, *Longing for an Absent God: Faith and Doubt in Great America Fiction*. Fortress Press, (March 2020).

44 Toni Morrison. *Beloved*. Knopf Doubleday Publishing. (Reprint Ed., 2004).

45 Joyce Marie Jackson, "Like a River Flowing with Living Water': *Worshipping in the Mississippi Delta*," *Folklife in Louisiana*. Virtual Books, Louisiana Division of the Arts, Louisiana Voices Folklife in Education Project, Online. ¶ 22.

46 Toni Morrison, *Beloved*.

47 Toni Morrison, Interview with David Carrasco. "Have Mercy: The Religious Dimensions of the Writings of Toni Morrison." Harvard Divinity School. Sperry Room. YouTube. December 6, 2013.

48 Joyce Marie Jackson, "Like a River Flowing with Living Water: Worshipping in the Mississippi Delta," ¶ 3.

49 Ted Ownby, *Mississippi Encyclopedia*, *Religion*. University of Mississippi, http://mississippiencyclopedia.org/overviews/religion/ February 2, 2018. Accessed June 28, 2024.

50 Richard Wright, *Black Boy*. Harper Perennial Modern Classics. 2008

51 Wright, Richard. *Black Boy*, chapter 5.

52 William Faulkner, *The Sound and the Fury*. Random House, The Modern Library Edition, (New York, 1992), 292.

53 Ted Ownby, *Mississippi Encyclopedia*, University of Mississippi, Center for the Study of Southern Culture.

54 Ownby, Ted. *Mississippi Encyclopedia*. University of Mississippi. Center for the Study of Southern Culture. http://mississippiencyclopedia.org/overviews/religion/.

55 Ownby.

56 Mark Tooley, "A Final Memoir of William Faulkner." *Juicy Ecumenism: The Institute on Religion and Democracy.* Online. December 17, 2012, ¶ 4

57 Jesmyn Ward, *Men We Reaped, A Memoir.* Bloomsbury, (New York, 2013), 110.

58 William Faulkner, *Light in August.* The Modern Library. (Toronto: Random House of Canada, 1959), 347.

59 Joyce Marie Jackson, "Like a River Flowing with Living Water: Worshiping in the Mississippi Delta." *Folklife in Louisiana.* "Like a River Flowing with Living Water: Worshiping in the Mississippi Delta" (louisianafolklife.org). Louisiana Division of the Arts.

60 Furry Lewis, In Cobb, James C. *The Most Sourthern Place on Earth.* Oxford Press (NYC, 1992), 295.

61 Walker Percy, *The Last Gentleman.*

62 William Alexander Percy, *Lantern on the Levee* (1941).

63 W. Ralph Eubanks, "Mississippi Delta: Returning Home to Its Haunted Past." Online. ¶ 14.

64 Cobb, *The Most Southern Place on Earth*, 324.

65 Cobb, *The Most Southern Place on Earth.*

66 Cobb, *The Most Southern Place on Earth*, 329.

67 Shelby Foote, *Tournament*, Summa Pubns., Second Edition, (June 25, 1987).

68 David L. Cohn, *Where I Was Born and Raised,* (Boston, 1948).

69 Shelby Foote, *The Civil War: A Narrative from Fredericksburg to Meridian* (New York, 1963), 63.

70 Mark Doty, "Souls on Ice," Poets.org. Online, July 18, 2000.

71 William Faulkner, *The Wild Palms.* Vintage International, (2011).

72 W. Ralph Eubanks, "Mississippi Delta," Online. ¶ 21.

73 Walker Percy, *The Last Gentleman from The Moviegoer, The Last Gentleman, The Second Coming.* Quality Paperback Book Club (New York, 1991).

74 Jesmyn Ward, *Men We Reaped, A Memoir.* (New York: Bloomsbury, 2013), 10.

75 Phillip Gordon, "The Delta and Yoknapatawpha: The Layering of Geography and Myth in the Works of William Faulkner," Center for the Study of Southern Culture. University of Mississippi, Online, November 28, 2016, ¶ 7.

76 Jesmyn Ward, *Men We Reaped, A Memoir,* (New York: Bloomsbury, 2013), 158.

77 Greg Iles, *Mississippi Blood.* William Morrow. 2017.
Iles' comments about the "blood with some river in it" inspired the title for this mosaic poem.

78 Cohn, *Where I Was Born and Raised*, 320.

79 Ralph Eubanks, *A Place Like Mississippi.*

80 Alan Lomax, "Land Where the Blues Began." 6; Lawrence Goodwyn, *The Populist Moment: A Short History of the Agrarian Revolt I America.* Oxford, (London, New York: 1978), 320.

81 Petty Betty, Int., Sorgel, Andrew. "Mississippi Yearning." U.S. News & World Report. 27 March. 2018. Online. ¶ 39.

82 Charles Bell, *The Married Land*, Houghton Mifflin Company, (Boston, 1962).

Jamie Tate has dedicated her life to making her mark as a Mississippi painter. Living and working in the very heart of the Mississippi Delta for most of her life, she found that the landscapes that surround her are what inspires and informs her work. Tate has received numerous awards for her art and continually presents her works at solo exhibits and group exhibits. She is a founding member of the Delta Artists Association in Mississippi, currently holds Board of Director seats on the Greenville Arts Council and the Mississippi Art Colony. She has previously held Board of Director seats for art associations in Texas and Arkansas, as well as in Mississippi. Tate has served as Exhibit Chair for the Greenville Arts Council and other art councils. She is a member of the Delta Artists Association, the Greenville Arts Council, and the Mississippi Art Colony, in addition to being a charter member of the Leland Blues Project, and the Highway 61 Blues Museum in Mississippi. Her professional artist website is found at www.jamietate.com She is an Art member of the National League of American Pen Women (NLAPW) and National board of directors member of that organization.

Tate studied Art Education at Delta State University, going on to further her studies through 45 years of painting workshops through the Mississippi Art Colony and others. This experience provided not only exposure to and input from many brilliant painting instructors, but also close relationships with other painters and their experience and expertise, as well as exhibiting opportunities. She was the recipient of a Professional Development Grant by the Mississippi Arts Commission in 2009, the Vinnie Ream National Award for Excellence in the Arts in 2019, and Best in Show in the 2024 National Museum of Women in the Arts, Mississippi Showcase. She has shown work in the National Art Club, New York City (2013) and in several group exhibits in Washington, D.C. Her paintings hang in corporate collections with Planters Bank, Prime Care Nursing, Inc., and the Museum of the Mississippi Delta among others, and in numerous private collections and with The Kennedy Center, Washington, D.C., and others throughout the south, nationally and internationally.

After living and painting in Stoneville, MS most of her life, she and her husband Bud, along with Gabbi the Labrador, relocated to just outside Indianola Mississippi, where her studio is located in the perfectly renovated loft of the barn overlooking the Delta landscape she loves.

Author and English educator **Nancy Avery Dafoe** writes across genres and has won multiple awards for her work, including the William Faulkner/William Wisdom creative writing competition in poetry (2016) and the national Soul Making Prose Poetry prize. She won first place in the international short story competition from New Century Writers, among other honors for her work. Dafoe has written sixteen published books, including her five collections of poetry (FLP), the most recent being this collection and *When Mine Canaries Stop Singing*. Her memoir on love, time, and grief about the loss of her son, *Unstuck in Time: A Memoir and Mystery on Loss and Love* was published in 2021, and her latest literary/historical novel is *Yet in the Land of the Living* (WingsePress, 2024). Her other novels include *Socrates is Dead Again* (PWP, 2022) and a murder mystery series *You Enter a Room, Both End in Speculation,* and *Murder on Ponte Vecchio* (RPP). Dafoe has also written about Alzheimer's disease and its effect on family in her memoir *An Iceberg in Paradise: A Passage Through Alzheimer's* (SUNY Press, 2015). Her contemporary fable/novella *Naimah and Ajmal on Newton's Mountain* (FLP) joins her other fiction work. In addition, Dafoe has written books on educational policy and teaching writing, published through Rowman & Littlefield *Education: Breaking Open the Box, The Misdirection of Education Policy,* and *Writing Creatively*.

Her fiction, poetry, and nonfiction works appear in a number of anthologies, including *Lost Orchard* (SUNY Press) and *Lost Orchard II* (PWP); *NY Votes for Women: A Suffrage Centennial Anthology* (Cayuga Lake Books); *Birdsong; Earth Care: Environment Problems and Possible Solutions; From the Finger Lakes, a Memoir Anthology,* and in numerous journals and literary magazines.

Numerous trips to and down the Mississippi River and the Delta region, in addition to her friendship with Mississippi artist Jamie Tate were the seeds of creation for this long form poem.

Dafoe has taught English and creative writing in a variety of settings, including high school, community college, and workshops. She continues to offer writing workshops and may be contacted through her website: nancydafoebooks.com or her email address; dafoe.nancy@gmail.com to discuss author talks for book clubs and other groups. She is a member of the Center for the Arts, and a board of directors' member of the National League of American Pen Women (NLAPW) and Central New York (CNY) Branch, in addition to being on the board for Cortland Arts Connect. She and her husband Daniel live on the shores of Little York Lake in Homer, New York with their dog Lincoln.

www.ingramcontent.com/pod-product-compliance
Lightning Source LLC
Chambersburg PA
CBHW040253170426
43191CB00019B/2402